RECIPES
from the
VINEYARDS
of
NORTHERN
CALIFORNIA

Main Courses

Leslie Mansfield

CELESTIALARTS
Berkeley, California

*When preparing recipes that call for egg yolks or whites, whether or not they are to be cooked, use only the highest quality, salmonella-free eggs.

CELESTIALARTS

P.O. Box 7123
Berkeley, California 94707

Distributed in Canada by Ten Speed Canada, in the United Kingdom and Europe by Airlift Books, in New Zealand by Southern Publishers Group, in Australia by Simon & Schuster Australia, in South Africa by Real Books, and in Singapore, Malaysia, Hong Kong, and Thailand by Berkeley Books.

Cover and interior design by Brad Greene
Cover photograph by Larry Kunkel
Photo styling by Veronica Randall
Public Domain Art thanks to Dover Publications

Library of Congress Card Catalog Number 99-70628

First printing, 1999
Printed in the United States

1 2 3 4 5 6 7 — 03 02 01 00 99

To Veronica Randall,
for teaching me so much.

ACKNOWLEDGMENTS

Deepest gratitude goes to my husband Richard, who has helped me with every step—his name belongs on the title page along with mine. To my wonderful parents, Stewart and Marcia Whipple, for their unflagging confidence. To my editor Veronica Randall, who is everything I could ever want in a friend. To my editor Heather Garnos, who helps keep it all together. To Brad Greene, for another spectacular design. To Larry Kunkel, for his glorious photography.

Finally, this book would not have been possible without the cooperation of the many people at the wineries who graciously contributed their favorite recipes. I wish to thank them all for their generosity.

Table of Contents

Introduction

Just mention California wine country and thoughts of warm sunshine, vines heavy with ripening grapes, and a relaxed lifestyle come to mind. The small villages throughout the wine country each have their own personalities, as do the wineries. From rural, family-run boutique wineries to large, stately wineries surrounded by a sea of vineyards, they all have one thing in common—a love for good food and wine.

This love of food and wine has resulted in an explosion of cutting-edge ideas that have defined California cuisine, incorporating the finest of Europe and Asia while drawing on the incredible local and seasonal bounty.

Entertaining is a way of life in wine country. Whether it is a formal dinner with many courses to showcase a variety of wines, or just drawing off a pitcher of new wine from the barrel to go with an impromptu picnic with neighbors, the desire to share the best they have to offer has helped shape the cuisine of California.

In the following pages you will find recipes offered from the finest wineries of northern California. Each is a reflection of their personality, whether formal or casual, and all are delicious. Each one is a taste of wine country.

1993
MENDOCINO
PETITE SIRAH
Upton Vineyards

GRAPES GROWN ORGANICALLY

CONTAINS NO DETECTABLE SULFITES
NO SULFITES ADDED
ALCOHOL 13.0% BY VOLUME

FREY VINEYARDS

A member of California Certified Organic Farmers, Frey Vineyards was one of the first to farm their vineyards organically and offer a wine from certified organically grown grapes. Located near the northernmost origins of the Russian River watershed, this Mendocino-appellation winery produces elegant, well-structured wines from its dry-farmed vineyards.

MARINATED TOFU
with Glazed Onions
& Pickled Ginger

*The garnish of chopped scallions lends
a textural counterpoint to the silky tofu.
Both vegetarians and meat eaters will
delight in this meatless entrée from chef
Tamara Frey.*

2 (14-ounce) packages extra-firm tofu, drained

1 cup Frey Vineyards Petite Syrah

3/4 cup honey

3 tablespoons soy sauce

2 tablespoons apple juice

2 tablespoons Dijon mustard

2 tablespoons sesame oil

2 cloves garlic, minced

4 white onions, thinly sliced

1 pound spaghetti

1/4 cup chopped scallions

1/4 cup sesame seeds, toasted

2 tablespoons pickled ginger

(recipe continued on next page)

Slice tofu crosswise into 6 pieces. Drain on paper towels. In a bowl, whisk together wine, honey, soy sauce, apple juice, mustard, sesame oil, and garlic. Pour into a 13 by 9-inch baking pan. Place the tofu slices in the pan in one layer. Cover tofu with the onion slices. Cover pan with foil and let marinate for 2 hours.

Preheat oven to 400° F. Place covered pan in oven and bake for 45 minutes. Remove foil and continue to bake an additional 20 minutes, or until marinade thickens and onions are well done. Remove from oven and carefully remove tofu and onions with a spatula. Reserve any additional cooking liquid.

Cook spaghetti in boiling salted water until al dente, then drain. Return spaghetti to pot. Pour reserved cooking liquid over spaghetti and stir gently until liquid is absorbed.

Divide spaghetti onto six plates and place 2 pieces of tofu with onions on top of each. Sprinkle scallions, sesame seeds, and pickled ginger on top.

Serves 6
Serve with Frey Vineyards
Petite Syrah

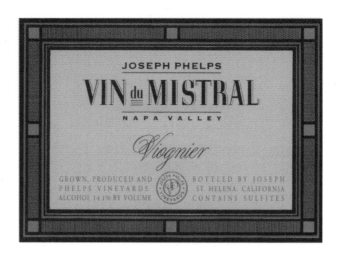

JOSEPH PHELPS
VINEYARDS

Few wineries in northern California have more "firsts" to their name than the winery of Joseph Phelps. Insignia, the first Bordeaux-style blend to be produced in California as a proprietary wine, ushered in the era of Meritage wines. His 1974 Syrah was perhaps the first time that variety had been bottled as such. And since 1990, his Vin du Mistral wines have epitomized the classic Rhone varietals. Located in a stunning redwood building, the winery is anchored to the landscape by a massive wisteria-covered trellis made from 100-year-old recycled bridge timbers. It is definitely worth an appointment to visit this pioneer of the modern Napa Valley.

TUNA FILLET
with Black Bean,
Mango & Papaya Salsa

This tasty and festive creation from chef
Trey Blankenship beautifully illustrates the
Hispanic influence on wine country cuisine.

BLACK BEAN, MANGO,
AND PAPAYA SALSA:

4 cups cooked black beans

1 small onion, finely chopped

$1/4$ cup diced mango

$1/4$ cup diced papaya

2 tablespoons minced garlic

1 serrano chile, minced

1 tablespoon minced cilantro

1 tablespoon freshly squeezed lime juice

1 tablespoon olive oil

Salt and freshly ground black pepper

4 (6-ounce) tuna fillets

Salt and white pepper

2 tablespoons whole coriander seeds

2 tablespoons whole cumin seeds

2 tablespoons whole fennel seeds

For the salsa: In a large bowl, combine all ingredients and toss gently. Cover and let sit at room temperature for 30 minutes.

For the tuna: Prepare the grill. Season the tuna with salt and white pepper. In a small sauté pan, combine coriander, cumin, and fennel. Sauté over medium heat just until spices start to pop. Grind spices coarsely in a mortar and pestle, then place them in a shallow dish. Press tuna fillets into spices, coating well on both sides. Grill about 5 minutes per side, or until fish just starts to flake. Do not overcook.

To serve, divide salsa onto four plates. Place a tuna fillet on top and serve immediately.

Serves 4
Serve with Joseph Phelps Vineyards
Viognier

Chandon Brut Cuvée 194 is a classic blend of 58% Pinot Noir, 24% Chardonnay, 11% Pinot Blanc and 7% Pinot Meunier.

CHANDON

Brut Cuvée

METHODE CHAMPENOISE

750 mL   12% alc./vol.

NAPA COUNTY 64% · SONOMA COUNTY 36% · SPARKLING WINE

DOMAINE CHANDON

California's first French-owned winery, and a leader in the development of sparkling wine in California, Domaine Chandon has been a forerunner in the art of pairing food and wine. Their on-site restaurant, using the freshest of local ingredients, along with inspiration from the entire Pacific Rim, has been instrumental in developing what is now known as California cuisine.

BLACK MUSSELS
Steamed in Chandon Brut

Robert Curry, executive chef at Domaine Chandon, adds a baguette and a tomato and mozzarella salad for a perfect light meal.

3/4 cup butter, divided

3 shallots, minced

2 cloves garlic, minced

3 cups Domaine Chandon Brut

3 tablespoons minced fresh thyme

4 1/2 pounds black mussels, scrubbed and debearded

1 cup chopped Italian parsley

1 tomato, peeled, seeded, and chopped

Juice of 2 lemons

In a large pot, melt 3 tablespoons of butter over medium heat. Add shallots and garlic and sauté until tender. Add wine and thyme and bring to a boil over high heat. Add mussels, cover, and steam for about 3 minutes until mussels open. Remove mussels to a large serving bowl. Discard any that do not open. Reduce heat to medium and whisk remaining butter into the simmering broth. Stir in parsley, tomato, and lemon juice and simmer 5 minutes. Pour broth over mussels and serve.

Serves 4
Serve with Domaine Chandon Brut

DRY FARMED

TOPOLOS
at Russian River Vineyards

Sonoma Mountain
Chardonnay
1994

HILLSIDE

PRODUCED & BOTTLED BY TOPOLOS
AT RUSSIAN RIVER VINEYARDS, FORESTVILLE, CA, USA
WITH ORGANICALLY GROWN GRAPES
ALCOHOL 13% BY VOLUME, CONTAINS SULFITES

TOPOLOS RUSSIAN RIVER VINEYARDS

Topolos Russian River Vineyards is a family-owned winery and restaurant in Sonoma County just an hour north of San Francisco and fifteen minutes west of Santa Rosa. Whether you choose to dine outside around the fountain patio or inside by the fireplace, Russian River Vineyards is the ultimate Sonoma County winery experience. The ambience is casual but elegant, and the menus combine authentic Greek cuisine from the Topolos family's recipes with offerings from the rest of the Mediterranean and the chef's creative inventions.

PRAWNS SANTORINI

The Greek isle of Thera, once known as Santorini, has lent its name to this Hellenic repast. One taste, and you'll want to break a crust of bread and dance in the streets.

1/4 cup olive oil

1 pound medium shelled shrimp

1 bunch scallions, chopped

1/2 cup Topolos Russian River Chardonnay

4 tomatoes, peeled, seeded, and chopped

6 ounces feta cheese, diced

1 1/2 tablespoons minced fresh dill

Hot cooked rice as an accompaniment

In a large skillet, heat olive oil over medium-high heat. Add shrimp and sauté until pink. With a slotted spoon, remove shrimp to a bowl. Add scallions to the skillet and sauté just until fragrant. Whisk in wine. Return shrimp to skillet and stir in tomatoes, feta, and dill. Cover and raise heat to high. Cook 3 minutes, remove lid and stir. Serve over rice.

Serves 4
Serve with Topolos Russian River Chardonnay

KENWOOD VINEYARDS

At Kenwood Vineyards, each vineyard lot is handled separately within the winery to preserve its individuality. Such "small lot" winemaking allows the winemaker to bring each lot of wine to its fullest potential. This style of winemaking is evident in the quality of Kenwood's special bottlings. From the Jack London Vineyard series, whose grapes come from the historical lava-terraced vineyards of the Jack London Ranch, to the Artist Series Cabernet Sauvignon, whose labels each year feature the work of a renowned artist, Kenwood's reds show Sonoma at its best.

PARCHMENT-BAKED SEA BASS *with Papaya, Pear & Mango Salsa*

*Follow executive chef Linda Kittler's recipe,
and enjoy the burst of aroma when you unwrap
these moist, tender fillets.*

PAPAYA, PEAR, AND MANGO SALSA:

1/4 cup diced pear

1/4 cup diced Mexican papaya

1/4 cup diced mango

1/4 cup finely chopped red onion

2 tablespoons minced cilantro

2 tablespoons freshly squeezed lime juice

2 teaspoons minced serrano chiles

1 teaspoon minced garlic

PARCHMENT-BAKED SEA BASS:

4 (12 by 16-inch) sheets of parchment or foil

4 (6-ounce) sea bass fillets

4 tablespoons olive oil

Salt and freshly ground black pepper

4 tablespoons Kenwood Sonoma County Chardonnay

8 thin slices of red onion

8 sprigs fresh dill

12 thin slices of lemon

12 tablespoons butter

Hot cooked rice as an accompaniment

(recipe continued on next page)   *13*

For the salsa: In a bowl, combine all ingredients and toss gently. Cover and chill 1 hour to let the flavors marry.

For the sea bass: Preheat oven to 475° F. Lightly oil a rimmed baking sheet. Place a sheet of parchment on a work surface. Fold in half and make a crease. Rub sea bass fillets with olive oil and season well with salt and pepper. Open parchment and place a sea bass fillet next to the center crease. Top each fillet with 1 tablespoon of wine, 2 slices of red onion, 2 sprigs of dill, 3 slices of lemon, and 3 tablespoons butter. Fold parchment over fish, and starting at one end, roll and pinch the edges together firmly to make a good seal. Place the packets on the prepared baking sheet and bake for 15 minutes. Remove from oven but do not open for an additional 10 minutes.

To serve, place rice on plates. Open packets and place the sea bass on a bed of rice. Drizzle juice from the packets over the fish. Top with the salsa.

Serves 4
Serve with Kenwood Vineyards
Sonoma County Chardonnay

DOMAINE CARNEROS

Designed after Château de la Marquetterie in Champagne, with its roots in the French house of Taittinger, Domaine Carneros is the only sparkling wine producer using exclusively Carneros grapes for their super-premium méthode-champenoise. Situated atop a knoll surrounded by its vineyards, the château commands a spectacular view of the rolling hills of Carneros. Pinot Noir and Chardonnay, along with a lesser amount of Pinot Meunier, serve as the basis of Domaine Carneros' elegant and delicate sparkling wines.

PAN-SEARED CHILEAN SEA BASS *with* *Orange-Basil Cream Sauce*

Chef Kyle MacDonald serves this quick and delicious dish with green beans tossed with slivered sundried tomatoes and garlic mashed potatoes.

ORANGE-BASIL CREAM SAUCE:

2 tablespoons butter

2 shallots, minced

1 clove garlic, minced

2 cups dry white wine

$2/3$ cup freshly squeezed orange juice

$1^1/2$ cups heavy cream

$1/8$ teaspoon cumin

2 teaspoons freshly squeezed lemon juice

Salt and freshly ground black pepper

12 fresh basil leaves, thinly sliced

4 (6-ounce) Chilean sea bass fillets

Salt and freshly ground black pepper

3 tablespoons olive oil

For the sauce: In a saucepan, heat butter over medium heat. Add shallots and garlic and sauté until fragrant. Add wine and orange juice and reduce until syrupy. Add cream and cumin and simmer until reduced by half. Whisk in lemon juice. Season with salt and pepper to taste. Stir in basil and keep warm.

For the sea bass: Preheat oven to 400° F. Season sea bass with salt and pepper. In an ovenproof skillet, heat olive oil over medium-high heat. Sear sea bass in hot oil for 2 to 3 minutes per side until crispy and golden. Place skillet in the oven and finish cooking the fish for about 8 minutes, or until it just flakes. Serve on top of a pool of sauce.

Serves 6
Serve with Domaine Carneros
Le Rêve Sparkling Wine

1996

MITSUKO'S VINEYARD
CHARDONNAY
CARNEROS • NAPA VALLEY

CLOS PEGASE WINERY

Driven by a desire to combine ancient traditions with modern technology, Jan Shrem founded Clos Pegase in 1983. His dream of creating a "temple to wine" has resulted in one of the most stunning and dramatic wineries in the Napa Valley. Surrounded by art, and described as "America's first monument to wine as art," Clos Pegase makes stylistic and elegant wines. Their grace does justice to the winery's namesake, Pegasus, the winged horse of Greek mythology whose hooves unleashed the sacred spring of the muses, which irrigated vines and inspired poets.

GRILLED HALIBUT
with Kiwi & Pineapple Relish

KIWI AND PINEAPPLE RELISH:

2 cups peeled and diced kiwi

1^1/2 cups peeled and diced pineapple

^{1}/2 cup diced red bell pepper

^{1}/4 cup diced red onion

1 tablespoon freshly squeezed lime juice

2 teaspoons minced fresh mint

2 teaspoons brown sugar

^{1}/2 teaspoon grated fresh ginger

4 (6-ounce) halibut steaks

1 tablespoon freshly squeezed lime juice

Salt and freshly ground black pepper

For the relish: In a bowl, combine kiwi, pineapple, bell pepper, onion, lime juice, mint, brown sugar, and ginger. Stir gently to mix well. Cover and chill at least 2 hours to allow flavors to marry.

For the halibut: Prepare the grill. Place steaks in a shallow dish and pour lime juice over them. Season with salt and pepper. Grill over hot coals for approximately 5 minutes per side, or until fish just flakes. Serve topped with the relish.

Serves 4
Serve with Clos Pegase Winery Mitsuko's Vineyard
Chardonnay

ST. SUPÉRY VINEYARDS AND WINERY

No visit to the Napa Valley would be complete without a visit to the St. Supéry Wine Discovery Center in Rutherford. A demonstration vineyard, galleries within the center filled with panoramic murals, and displays all illustrate the lore of the vine. Both self-guided and guided tours serve to introduce the visitor to the wines and philosophy of St. Supéry.

CHILEAN SEA BASS
with Tropical Fruit Salsa & Tortillas

Chef Sunny Cristadoro has created an amazing combination of flavors, aromas, and textures. Feel free to add or substitute whatever fresh fruits might be in season.

5 (6-inch) flour tortillas
Salt

TROPICAL FRUIT SALSA:
1 mango, peeled and diced
1 peach, peeled and diced
1 pear, peeled, cored, and diced
2 kiwis, peeled and diced
1/2 cup diced pineapple
1/2 cup finely chopped red onion
1 tablespoon minced cilantro
1 tablespoon freshly squeezed lemon juice
1 tablespoon freshly squeezed lime juice
1 tablespoon St. Supéry Vineyards Sauvignon Blanc
2 teaspoons minced fresh ginger

1 cup St. Supéry Vineyards Sauvignon Blanc
6 (4-ounce) Chilean sea bass fillets
Salt and freshly ground black pepper

6 cups mixed greens

(recipe continued on next page)

🍂 Preheat oven to 350° F. Slice each tortilla into 6 equal triangles. Place on cookie sheet and sprinkle with salt. Bake for about 5 minutes or until crisp. Set aside.

For the salsa: In a large bowl, combine all ingredients and stir gently. Set aside.

For the sea bass: In a skillet just large enough to hold the fish, bring the wine to a simmer over medium heat. Season the sea bass with salt and pepper. Place fish in pan and poach for about 8 minutes, or until cooked through.

Place the mixed greens in a large bowl. Drain the salsa and reserve the liquid. Pour the salsa liquid over the greens and toss. Divide the greens onto six plates. Place sea bass fillet on top of greens. Top with a spoonful of salsa. Arrange 5 tortilla chips on each plate.

Serves 6
Serve with St. Supéry Vineyards
Sauvignon Blanc

MONTICELLO
VINEYARDS

Monticello, a 20,000-case winery just north of the town of Napa, was built in the style of Thomas Jefferson's personal estate in recognition of his contribution to American wine and food. Winery founder Jay Corley's family traces its connection back to 1640, and to Bedford County, Virginia, the same county where Jefferson advocated freedom for a new America. The Jefferson House at Monticello Vineyards stands as a symbol of excellence and quality in winemaking. The Oak Knoll region north of the town of Napa is home to Monticello's Chardonnay and Pinot Noir. Corley chose that area to plant Burgundian varieties because it is cooler than the upper valley; he reserves his State Lane Vineyard further north in warmer Yountville to plant Cabernet Sauvignon.

TUNISIAN FISH
with Harissa Marinade

The harissa gives a wonderfully searing heat to this variation of a classic North African preparation from chef David Lawson.

HARISSA:

9 dried New Mexico chiles

3 cloves garlic, minced

1/4 teaspoon caraway seeds, finely ground

1/8 teaspoon coriander

1/8 teaspoon salt

1/3 cup olive oil

1 onion, chopped

2 ounces fresh spinach, chopped

2 cloves garlic, minced

1/4 cup harissa

1 teaspoon salt

1 1/4 pounds red snapper or halibut fillets

For the harissa: Prepare the chiles by removing the stems and seeds. Tear the chiles into 1-inch pieces and place in a bowl. Cover with cold water and let soften for 15 minutes. Drain chiles well and pat dry. In the bowl of a food processor, combine chilies, garlic, caraway, coriander, and salt and process until smooth, scraping sides often. With the motor running, add oil in a thin stream until all is incorporated and it forms a smooth paste.

For the fish: In a bowl, stir together the onion, spinach, garlic, 1/4 cup of the harissa, and salt. Cut the fish into 4 pieces and place in heatproof pan or dish just large enough to hold the fish in one layer. Spread the onion mixture evenly over the fish. Put a steamer rack in a large kettle and add enough water to reach just below the bottom of the rack. Set the heatproof pan on the rack. Cover tightly and bring to a boil. Reduce heat to medium-low and steam the fish for about 15 minutes, or until it just flakes. Serve on a bed of couscous and vegetables and pass remaining harissa at the table.

Serves 4
Serve with Monticello Vineyards
Corley Reserve Merlot

V. SATTUI WINERY

V. Sattui Winery is a family-owned winery established in 1885, and located in St. Helena, the very heart of California's famous Napa Valley. Their award-winning wines are sold exclusively at the winery, by mail order, and from their website direct to customers. Surrounding the beautiful stone winery is a large tree-shaded picnic ground. V. Sattui also boasts a large gourmet cheese shop and deli.

STEAMED WHOLE ROCKFISH
with Ginger

*In its beautiful presentation and the
bright aromas of ginger and sesame, this
dish is reminiscent of the Far East.*

1 (2^1/2 to 3-pound) fancy rockfish,
    cleaned and with the head left on

8 thin slices fresh ginger

12 sprigs cilantro

1 cup finely shredded scallions

^{1}/3 cup finely shredded fresh ginger

^{1}/3 cup finely shredded red bell pepper

^{1}/4 cup finely shredded Anaheim chile

^{1}/4 cup vegetable oil

1 tablespoon cornstarch

^{1}/4 cup cold water

1 cup chicken stock

1 teaspoon salt

^{1}/2 teaspoon freshly ground black pepper

1 tablespoon sesame oil

(recipe continued on next page)

Rinse the fish inside and out and pat dry. Extend the belly cavity by cutting about a third of the way to the tail. Spread cavity apart and place belly-side-down in a heatproof dish. Make 4 vertical cuts on each side of the fish and insert slices of ginger. Sprinkle cilantro over fish.

Put a steamer rack in a large kettle and add enough water to reach just below the bottom of the rack. Set the heatproof dish on the rack. Cover tightly and bring to a boil. Reduce heat to medium-low and steam the fish for about 20 minutes, or until it just flakes.

Transfer fish to a warm and deep serving platter. Scatter half of the scallions, ginger, bell pepper, and chile over the fish. In a small saucepan, bring the oil to a boil. Pour the hot oil over the fish. Dissolve cornstarch in the cold water and pour into small saucepan. Whisk in the chicken stock, salt, and pepper. Bring to a boil, whisking constantly, and simmer until slightly thickened. Whisk in sesame oil and pour the hot liquid over the fish. Sprinkle remaining scallions, ginger, bell pepper, and chile over the fish and serve immediately.

Serves 4
Serve with V. Sattui Winery
Chardonnay

Cakebread Cellars

CARNEROS
Pinot Noir
1996

ALCOHOL 14.5% BY VOLUME

CAKEBREAD CELLARS

A true family winery, Cakebread Cellars in Rutherford is one of the most creative and successful wineries in California's famed Napa Valley. Since its founding in 1973, the winery has developed a reputation for producing world-class wines and pairing them with outstanding cuisine. Dolores Cakebread, the winery's culinary director, had the vision to plant vegetable gardens at the same time their vineyards were being planted. She has been a forerunner in the development of California cuisine, which emphasizes fresh, natural, and locally grown produce to complement the wines of Cakebread Cellars.

SALMON *with* CRISPY POTATO CRUST

1 potato

6 (5-ounce) salmon fillets, skin removed

Salt and freshly ground black pepper

3 tablespoons vegetable oil

ROASTED GARLIC MASHED POTATOES:

1 head garlic

1 tablespoon olive oil

2$\frac{1}{2}$ pounds russet potatoes, scrubbed

1 cup milk

$\frac{1}{4}$ cup butter

PINOT NOIR SAUCE:

4 cups Cakebread Cellars Pinot Noir

2 shallots, minced

2 cups veal stock

Trim the potato to form a cylinder. Slice potato into paper-thin disks, using a mandoline slicer if possible. Blanch in boiling water for 10 seconds. With a slotted spoon, remove potatoes and drop into an ice bath. Drain potato slices well and arrange over the top of salmon fillets to imitate fish scales. Refrigerate while making mashed potatoes and sauce.

For the potatoes: Preheat oven to 400° F. Remove the papery outer skins from garlic, leaving whole head intact. Slice 1/4 inch off the top. Place in the middle of a piece of foil and drizzle with olive oil. Bake for about 1 hour or until garlic is very tender. Remove from oven and cool. Squeeze garlic from skins. Place potatoes in a large pot and cover with cold water. Bring to a boil, then reduce heat to medium and simmer until they can be easily pierced with a knife. Drain and peel while still hot, but cool enough to handle. Cut into chunks and pass through a food mill with the roasted garlic into a pot. Return pot to stove and, over medium-high heat, stir in the milk and butter. Season with salt and pepper and keep warm over low heat.

For the sauce: In a saucepan, combine wine and shallots. Simmer over medium heat until syrupy. Stir in the veal stock and reduce by half. Strain and reserve.

For the salmon: Remove salmon from refrigerator and season with salt and pepper. In a large non-stick skillet, heat the oil over medium-high heat. Carefully place the salmon fillets in the skillet, potato-side-down. Cook until evenly browned. Turn over and cook on the other side until done. Serve salmon on top of mashed potatoes surrounded with the sauce.

Serves 6
Serve with Cakebread Cellars
Pinot Noir

SHAFER VINEYARDS

Located in the heart of the Stags Leap District of the Napa Valley, Shafer Vineyards has become synonymous with the finest the Napa Valley has to offer. Since their first crush in 1978, John Shafer and his son Doug have presided over the slow but steady growth of their premium winery, from the first 1000-case production to its present size. Highly acclaimed by colleagues within the wine industry, the wines from Shafer Vineyards reflect their terroir through their complex spectrum of aromas and flavors.

GRATINÉED SALMON

This spicy coating keeps the salmon exceptionally moist. Panko bread crumbs can be found at Asian grocery stores.

1 (2-pound) salmon fillet

Salt and freshly ground black pepper

2 tablespoons prepared horseradish

2 tablespoons minced fresh parsley

2 tablespoons freshly grated Parmesan cheese

1 tablespoon melted butter

1 tablespoon honey

1 tablespoon Dijon mustard

1 teaspoon cider vinegar

2 cups panko bread crumbs

Preheat oven to 350° F. Lightly oil a baking dish. Place salmon in baking dish and season with salt and pepper.

In a bowl, whisk together horseradish, parsley, Parmesan, butter, honey, mustard, and vinegar until well blended. Stir in panko until evenly moistened. Pat mixture on top of salmon. Bake for about 30 to 40 minutes, or until salmon is cooked through.

Serves 6
Serve with Shafer Vineyards Merlot

BERINGER VINEYARDS

The oldest continually operating winery in the Napa Valley was started in 1876, by Jacob and Frederick Beringer, immigrants from Mainz, Germany. Currently a publicly traded company, owned by thousands of wine-loving shareholders, Beringer Vineyards excels in the production of vineyard-designated reds, graceful and supple whites, as well as lovingly tended, late harvest dessert wines.

PAN-ROASTED SALMON *with Pesto on Mashed Potatoes & Shiitake-Cabernet Gravy*

Beringer's chef Jerry Comfort created this winning combination of Cabernet with salmon. The year-round availability of fresh salmon and shiitake mushrooms makes this dish a treat in any season.

SHIITAKE AND CABERNET GRAVY:

3 cups chicken stock

1 cup Beringer Vineyards Knights Valley Cabernet Sauvignon

2 tablespoons minced shallots

1 tablespoon butter

6 shiitake mushrooms, caps only, sliced

Salt and freshly ground black pepper

PESTO:

1 bunch basil, leaves only

2 tablespoons freshly grated Parmesan cheese

1 clove garlic, minced

1/2 teaspoon salt

1/4 cup olive oil

(recipe continued on next page)

MASHED POTATOES:

1 tablespoon olive oil

1 bunch leeks, white part only, finely chopped

3 russet potatoes, peeled and quartered

3 tablespoons butter

3 tablespoons heavy cream

Salt and freshly ground black pepper

3 tablespoons vegetable oil

4 (6-ounce) salmon steaks

Salt and freshly ground black pepper

For the gravy: In a saucepan, bring chicken stock to a boil over medium heat. Simmer until it is reduced to 1 cup. In a small saucepan, combine wine with shallots and simmer over medium heat until reduced to about $1/4$ cup. Strain mixture into the chicken stock and discard solids. In a sauté pan, melt butter over medium heat. Add mushrooms and sauté until tender. Stir mushrooms into chicken stock mixture. Season with salt and pepper and keep warm.

For the pesto: In the bowl of a food processor, combine basil, Parmesan, garlic, and salt and process until smooth, scraping sides often. With the motor running, add olive oil in a thin stream until all is incorporated. Set aside.

For the potatoes: In a sauté pan, heat olive oil over medium heat. Add leeks and sauté until tender. Set aside. In a large pot, cook potatoes in salted water until tender. Drain potatoes and add reserved leeks, butter, and cream. Mash until smooth. Season with salt and pepper.

For the salmon: In a large cast-iron skillet, heat the vegetable oil over medium-high heat. Season the salmon with salt and pepper. Place salmon in hot skillet and cook for about 5 minutes, or until browned and crispy. Turn salmon and cook about 3 minutes, or until salmon just flakes.

To serve, divide mashed potatoes onto four plates. Top with a salmon steak. Put a dollop of pesto on salmon and spoon gravy around the potatoes.

Serves 4
Serve with Beringer Vineyards Knights Valley
Cabernet Sauvignon

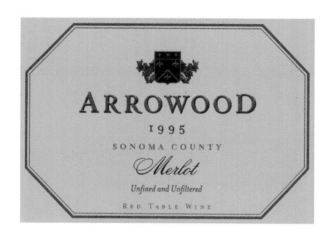

ARROWOOD VINEYARDS
AND WINERY

Richard Arrowood, one of California's most renowned winemakers, and his wife and partner Alis Demers Arrowood, have crafted a winery that sits in perfect harmony with its environs. Fashioned after a New England farmhouse, the winery has often been described as a "winemaker's dream." Home to a number of wonderful, rare, and outstanding wines, Arrowood uses an intimate knowledge of the Sonoma Valley's many microclimates and terroirs to create great and complex wines.

COQ AU VIN

The inclusion of potatoes in this classic Burgundian dish is a delicious variation. Make sure to have lots of crusty peasant bread to mop up the sauce.

6 slices bacon, chopped

1 chicken, cut into serving pieces

2 tablespoons butter

8 mushrooms, halved if large

16 pearl onions, peeled

2/3 cup chopped scallions

1 clove garlic, minced

2 1/2 tablespoons flour

1 teaspoon salt

1/4 teaspoon freshly ground black pepper

1/4 teaspoon thyme

2 cups Arrowood Vineyards Merlot

1 cup chicken stock

8 small new potatoes, scrubbed well

Chopped parsley for garnish

(recipe continued on next page)

 Preheat oven to 350° F.

In a Dutch oven, cook the bacon over medium heat until crisp. Add chicken and brown well on both sides. With a slotted spoon, remove chicken and bacon and set aside. Pour off all but 1 table-spoon of the drippings. Add butter, mushrooms, and pearl onions and sauté until lightly browned. Remove vegetables and set aside. Add scallions and garlic and sauté until fragrant. Whisk in flour, salt, pepper, and thyme and cook for 2 minutes. Whisk in wine and chicken stock. Return chicken, bacon, mushrooms, and pearl onions to the Dutch oven. Add the potatoes. Cover and bake for 1 hour. Remove lid and continue to bake for an additional 30 to 45 minutes, or until chicken is very tender and liquid is reduced. Serve in shallow bowls with lots of broth, garnished with parsley.

Serves 4 to 6
Serve with Arrowood Vineyards
Merlot

Napa Valley
FUMÉ BLANC
Dry Sauvignon Blanc
1996

PRODUCED AND BOTTLED BY GRGICH HILLS CELLAR
RUTHERFORD, CA · ALC. 12.8% BY VOL. · CONTAINS SULFITES

GRGICH HILLS
CELLAR

Grgich Hills Cellar, a collaboration between Miljenko Grgich and Austin Hills of the Hills Bros. Coffee family, has become known as the producer of big, mouth-filling Chardonnays, which connoisseurs consider to be among the finest in the world.

In addition to their incomparable Chardonnays, Grgich Hills produces a lush and firm Cabernet Sauvignon from estate vineyards in Yountville, as well as a delightfully clean and fruity Fumé Blanc from their Olive Hills estate vineyard. Of particular interest are their dry-farmed Zinfandels, grown on hot and windy hillside vineyard sites. These massive wines have impressive fruit and longevity.

LEMON CHICKEN

Aromatic jasmine rice would be an ideal side dish for this tangy summer recipe.

LEMON MARINADE:

1 cup Grgich Hills Cellar Fumé Blanc

Juice of 2 lemons

6 cloves garlic, halved

4 skinless and boneless chicken breasts

1 tablespoon olive oil

Salt and freshly ground black pepper

1 red bell pepper, sliced

8 ounces mushrooms, quartered

1 (6-ounce) jar marinated artichoke hearts,
    drained and quartered

1 tablespoon chopped fresh basil

1 tablespoon chopped fresh cilantro

1 tablespoon chopped fresh parsley

In a dish just large enough to hold the chicken, stir together the wine, lemon juice, and garlic. Place chicken in marinade and marinate 2 hours. Remove chicken and pat dry. Reserve marinade.

In a skillet, heat the olive oil over medium-high heat. Season the chicken breasts on both sides with salt and pepper. Add the chicken and cook until golden brown on both sides. Remove chicken to a heatproof serving platter and put in a warm oven. With a slotted spoon, remove garlic from marinade and add to the skillet. Sauté until fragrant. Add bell pepper and sauté until barely tender. Add mushrooms and sauté until tender. Add artichoke hearts and sauté until tender. Arrange the vegetables around the chicken and keep warm.

In a saucepan, bring reserved marinade to a boil over medium-high heat. Simmer until mixture is reduced by half. Pour over the chicken and vegetables and serve immediately.

Serves 4
Serve with Grgich Hills Cellar
Fumé Blanc

FROG'S LEAP WINERY

A strong commitment to sustainable agriculture along with the winery's goal of having fun explains much of what Frog's Leap stands for. After founding the winery in 1981, on a site known as the Frog Farm, John and Julie Williams rebuilt the century-old winery building into the home of some of the Napa Valley's finest wines. The winery's motto—"Time's fun when you're having flies"—reflects the tongue-in-cheek approach John and Julie take toward producing their excellent wines.

ROASTED CHICKEN

Delicious in its simplicity, this variation
of a classic is guaranteed to please.

1/2 cup Frog's Leap Winery Chardonnay

5 cloves garlic, lightly smashed

1 (4-pound) roasting chicken, preferably free range

Salt and freshly ground black pepper

1 bunch fresh tarragon

1 lemon, quartered

Preheat oven to 350° F. Lightly oil a roasting pan just large enough to hold the chicken. Combine wine and garlic in the roasting pan and place in oven for 10 minutes.

Season the chicken well inside and out with salt and pepper. Loosen the skin over the breast by carefully separating the skin from the meat with your fingers. Stuff each side with 2 sprigs of tarragon. Place lemon and 4 sprigs of tarragon inside the cavity of the chicken and truss.

Remove pan from oven and place chicken in the pan. Roast for 1 hour, basting every 10 minutes. Remove from oven and let sit for 10 minutes before carving.

Serves 4 to 6
Serve with Frog's Leap Winery
Chardonnay

VIANSA WINERY

On the evening of January 29, 1988, on a hill near Sonoma, Sam and Vicki Sebastiani opened a bottle of sparkling wine and toasted the land that would one day see their dream a reality. Their winery, Viansa, would embody a proud Italian heritage, and it would overlook a lowland shared by vineyards and nearly 100 acres of restored natural wetlands. Today, Viansa is a reality welcoming visitors from around the world, and they invite you to share your wedding, special event, or meeting with them. The wines and food of Viansa are among the world's finest, and the wetlands provide critical habitat to countless waterfowl, animals, and aquatic life.

CHICKEN SALTIMBOCCA
with Pesto Sauce

Saltimbocca usually refers to a complex and delicious veal dish, meaning literally "jump in the mouth." This pesto-flavored version was devised using chicken for a change of pace. This recipe is from **Cucina Viansa** *by Vicki Sebastiani.*

PESTO:

1 cup fresh basil leaves

1 cup Italian parsley

8 cloves garlic

1/3 cup olive oil

2 tablespoons freshly grated Parmesan cheese

2 tablespoons chopped walnuts

1/4 teaspoon salt

1/8 teaspoon freshly ground black pepper

CHICKEN SALTIMBOCCA:

8 large chicken thighs, boned with skin left on

8 very thin slices fontina cheese, cut to the size of the boned and opened thighs

8 very thin slices prosciutto, cut to the size of the boned and opened thighs

Salt and freshly ground black pepper

(recipe continued on next page)

SAUCE:

1 cup heavy cream

🍇 Preheat oven to 375° F. Lightly oil an 8 by 8-inch baking dish.

For the pesto: In the bowl of a food processor, combine basil, parsley, garlic, olive oil, Parmesan, walnuts, salt, and pepper and process until smooth.

For the chicken: Lay out each chicken thigh, skin-side-down. Spread each thigh with about 2 tablespoons pesto (reserve remaining pesto for the sauce) and top with a slice of cheese and a slice of proscuitto. Roll up each thigh to enclose filling and place tightly together, seam-side-down, in prepared baking dish. Season with salt and pepper and bake uncovered for 30 minutes.

For the sauce: In a bowl, whip the cream until thickened. Fold in the reserved pesto. Cover and keep at room temperature until ready for use.

To serve, transfer chicken thighs to a serving platter and top with sauce.

Serves 8
Serve with Viansa Winery
Nebbiolo

KORBEL CHAMPAGNE CELLARS

Located just east of Guerneville and just a handful of miles inland from the Pacific Ocean, Korbel Champagne Cellars is a name that has stood for fine méthode-champenoise sparkling wines for over a hundred years. Founded in the late 1880's by three immigrant brothers from Bohemia—Francis, Anton, and Joseph Korbel—and owned and managed by the Heck family since 1954, Korbel has developed into one of California's most respected champagne houses.

CHICKEN FETA
with Lemon Tarragon Cream Sauce

Chef Phil McGauley of Korbel Champagne Cellars has created this tangy sauce, which perfectly showcases the delicacy of their fine champagne.

LEMON TARRAGON CREAM SAUCE:

1 tablespoon butter

8 mushrooms, sliced

2 tablespoons finely chopped shallots

Zest of 2 lemon, minced

1 tablespoon tarragon vinegar

1 tablespoon cracked black peppercorns

2 bay leaves

2 cups Korbel Champagne Cellars
   Chardonnay Champagne

1 cup chicken stock

2 cups heavy cream

Juice of 2 lemons

1 tablespoon finely chopped fresh tarragon

1/2 teaspoon salt

6 skinless and boneless chicken breasts

Salt and freshly ground black pepper

1 cup all-purpose flour

2 tablespoons olive oil

1 cup Korbel Champagne Cellars Chardonnay
   Champagne

1/2 cup seeded and chopped tomatoes

1/2 cup chopped scallions

1/2 cup chopped Kalamata olives

1 cup feta cheese, crumbled

2 tablespoons chopped fresh tarragon, for garnish

For the sauce: In a saucepan, melt butter over
medium heat. Add mushrooms and shallots and
sauté until tender. Stir in lemon zest, vinegar, peppercorns, and bay leaves and cook for 1 minute. Stir
in wine and stock and simmer until mixture is
reduced by half. Stir in cream and lemon juice and
simmer until mixture is reduced by half. Whisk in
tarragon and salt and keep warm.

For the chicken: Season chicken breasts with
salt and pepper. Lightly dredge in flour and shake
off the excess. In a large skillet, heat olive oil over
medium heat. Add chicken and cook until nicely
browned. Turn chicken over and add wine. Cover
and cook for about 10 minutes or until cooked
through. Serve topped with tomatoes, scallions, and
olives. Pour lemon cream sauce over and garnish
with tarragon.

Serves 6
Serve with Korbel Champagne Cellars
Chardonnay Champagne

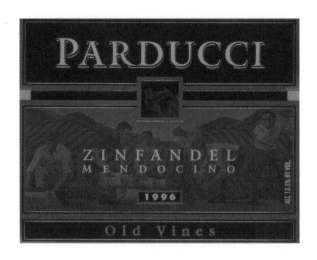

PARDUCCI WINE ESTATES

There are only two things you need to know about a wine. First, do you like it? Second, can you afford it? The people at Parducci are confident that, after tasting and pricing Parducci wines, the answer to both questions will be an emphatic "yes." They have always recognized that wine customers enjoy a variety of wines. As such, they have taken advantage of the numerous varieties grown in Mendocino County and now produce all the following: Cabernet Sauvignon, Chenin Blanc, Pinot Noir, Chardonnay, Charbono, Barbera, Petite Sirah, Merlot, Sauvignon Blanc, Zinfandel, Syrah, and Sangiovese. Parducci strives to bring out the varietal characteristics each grape has to offer, and believes that wine is an honest, natural product that should never be over-processed.

SPICY BLACKBERRY & GINGER CHICKEN

1 cup seedless blackberry jam

$1/2$ cup freshly squeezed orange juice

$1/2$ cup Parducci Wine Estates Zinfandel

1 bunch scallions, chopped

2 tablespoons soy sauce

2 teaspoons minced fresh ginger

$1/4$ teaspoon cayenne pepper

1 chicken, cut up

Salt and freshly ground black pepper

Preheat oven to 350° F. Lightly oil an 8 by 8-inch baking dish.

In a saucepan, whisk together blackberry jam, orange juice, wine, scallions, soy sauce, ginger, and cayenne pepper. Bring to a simmer over medium heat and continue to whisk until smooth. Simmer for 5 minutes.

Place chicken, skin-side-up, in one layer in prepared baking dish. Season with salt and pepper. Pour blackberry sauce over chicken. Bake for 1 hour, basting occasionally. Serve over rice with sauce spooned on top.

Serves 6
Serve with Parducci Wine Estates
Zinfandel

1997
ANDERSON VALLEY
GEWURZTRAMINER

GROWN, PRODUCED AND BOTTLED BY THE H.A. OSWALD FAMILY
PHILO, CA. ALCOHOL 12.85% BY VOLUME, RESIDUAL SUGAR 0.8%

HUSCH VINEYARDS

Husch Vineyards is a small family winery and the first bonded winery located in the Anderson Valley appellation of Mendocino County in northern California, a picturesque two-and-a-half hour drive north of San Francisco. All Husch wines are made from grapes grown in the family-owned vineyards. Some of the wines are distributed throughout the United States, but many are available only locally or at their tasting room. Quality is the key word at the winery. It shows in the care that goes into growing fine grapes, in the attention given in each step of the winemaking process, and in the time given to visitors who come to the winery for tastings.

MALAYSIAN CHICKEN CURRY

Delightful in its subtlety, this rich curry is a perfect foil for the complexities of an aromatic Gewürztraminer.

2 tablespoons vegetable oil

1 small onion, chopped

1 tablespoon curry powder

1 tablespoon minced garlic

1 (14-ounce) can unsweetened coconut milk

1 cup chopped tomatoes

4 boneless and skinless chicken breasts, cut into 1-inch cubes

4 waxy potatoes, peeled and cut into 1-inch cubes

In a heavy Dutch oven, heat oil over medium heat. Add the onion and sauté until translucent. Sprinkle the curry powder and garlic over the onions and sauté until fragrant. Stir in coconut milk and tomatoes until blended. Stir in chicken and potatoes. Reduce heat to medium-low, cover, and simmer for 30 minutes. Remove lid and simmer an additional 10 minutes to reduce the liquid. Serve over rice.

Serves 4
Serve with Husch Vineyards
Gewürztraminer

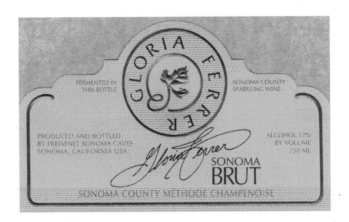

GLORIA FERRER
CHAMPAGNE CAVES

Founded by José Ferrer, son of Pedro Ferrer Bosch, the Spanish-Catalan founder of Freixenet, Gloria Ferrer Champagne Caves was opened to the public in July of 1986. Named for José Ferrer's beloved wife, Gloria, the winery has been winning awards and the accolades of wine critics ever since. Located within the cool Carneros appellation, the beautiful building with stucco walls, arched windows, and overhanging balconies is a piece of the proud history of old Spain.

SPARKLING CHICKEN

Although the bubbles sadly leave during cooking, the delicacy of the sparkling wine remains in this elegant main course.

1 free-range chicken, cut into 8 pieces

1 bottle Gloria Ferrer Champagne Caves Sonoma Brut

Salt and freshly ground black pepper

Flour for dredging

3 tablespoons olive oil

2 leeks, white and pale green part only, chopped

1 onion, chopped

1 carrot, chopped

1 stalk celery, chopped

2 cloves garlic, minced

1/2 cup chopped parsley

1 tomato, peeled, seeded, and chopped

2 tablespoons chopped fresh thyme

1 tablespoon all-purpose flour

3 tablespoons chicken stock

(recipe continued on next page)

In a deep bowl, combine chicken and wine. Cover and refrigerate overnight.

Preheat oven to 350° F. Lightly oil a 9 by 13-inch baking dish. With a slotted spoon, remove chicken from the wine and pat dry. Reserve wine. Season chicken with salt and pepper. Lightly dredge in flour and shake off the excess. In a large skillet, heat olive oil over medium heat. Add chicken and brown well on both sides. Remove chicken and place skin-side-up in prepared baking dish. Set aside.

Pour off all but 2 tablespoons of fat from the skillet. Add leeks, onion, carrot, celery, and garlic and sauté until tender. Add parsley, tomato, and thyme and sauté 3 minutes. Sprinkle 1 tablespoon flour over vegetables and stir until well mixed. Stir in reserved wine and chicken stock. Simmer until liquid is reduced by half. Strain mixture and discard solids. Pour broth over the chicken. Bake for 1 hour, or until chicken is cooked and broth is slightly thickened. Serve chicken over rice and spoon broth on top.

Serves 4 to 6
Serve with Gloria Ferrer Champagne Caves Sonoma Brut

DUCKHORN VINEYARDS

When your last name is Duckhorn, it stands to reason that you would choose a duck to be a symbol for your winery. Dan and Margaret Duckhorn have taken that theme and created one of the Napa Valley's most respected premium wineries. Hand-harvested and sorted grapes enter their crusher to emerge as ultra-premium Cabernets, Merlots, Zinfandels, and Sauvignon Blancs. New vineyards in Mendocino's Anderson Valley promise to deliver world-class Pinot Noirs to their flock of stylistic wines.

WILD DUCK
with Port Sauce

A panoply of complex flavors come together in this wonderful sauce, which serves to bring out every ounce of the duck's inherent flavor.

1 bottle California port

1 cup freshly squeezed orange juice

Juice of 1 lemon

$1/4$ cup chopped red onion

3 tablespoons chopped red bell pepper

2 cloves garlic, minced

2 tablespoons blackberry jam

1 tablespoon peach chutney

1 tablespoon liquid beef bouillon (Bovril)

$1^1/2$ teaspoons Worcestershire sauce

$1/2$ cup cold butter, cut into small pieces

Salt and freshly ground black pepper

1 tablespoon chopped fresh parsley

3 wild ducks (or 2 domestic ducks), cut in half along the backbone

Salt and freshly ground black pepper

In a saucepan, combine port, orange juice, and lemon juice. Simmer over medium heat for 15 minutes. Stir in onion, bell pepper, garlic, blackberry jam, chutney, bouillon, and Worcestershire sauce. Reduce heat to low and reduce by half. Strain and discard solids. Return port mixture to saucepan and continue to simmer over low heat until very thick. Add butter, a little at a time, whisking well to incorporate after each addition. Season with salt and pepper and stir in parsley. Place sauce in the top of a double boiler over warm, not simmering, water. Do not let sauce get too warm or it will separate.

Prepare the grill. Season duck halves with salt and pepper. Place on grill, skin-side-down, until well browned. Turn over and grill until done. Spoon sauce over sliced duck.

Serves 6 to 8
Serve with Duckhorn Vineyards Estate
Merlot

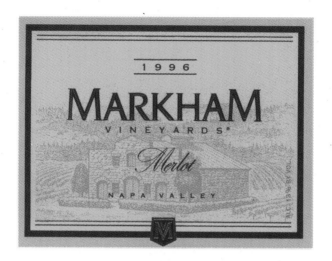

MARKHAM VINEYARDS

Markham Vineyards has, for over twenty years, rewarded oenophiles with wines of a consistency and level of quality seldom matched in the Napa Valley. From its historic stone winery, built in 1873 by Jean Laurent, an immigrant from Bordeaux, Markham crafts outstanding wines that are unpretentious in style and are meant to be enjoyed. Vineyards from San Pablo Bay north to Calistoga provide a wealth of different growing conditions for both their white and red wines.

GRILLED DUCK BREAST *on Creamy Polenta with Port & Sundried Cherries*

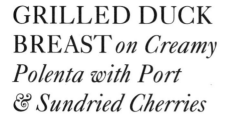

In this elegant dish from Linda Thomas Catering, the creamy polenta lends a glorious harmony to the flavors of the rich Muscovy duck and the piquant cherry port sauce.

PORT AND SUNDRIED CHERRY SAUCE:

8 ounces sundried cherries

$1/4$ cup port

$1/3$ cup water

$1/4$ cup chicken stock

$1/4$ cup raspberry vinegar

$1/4$ cup butter

$1/4$ cup minced shallots

2 cups heavy cream

Salt and freshly ground black pepper

ROASTED GARLIC PURÉE:

4 heads garlic

$1/3$ cup melted butter

$1/3$ cup olive oil

Salt and freshly ground black pepper

(recipe continued on next page)

CREAMY POLENTA:

3 cups chicken stock

1 cup heavy cream

1 cup water

3 tablespoons roasted garlic purée

1 teaspoon salt

1 cup cornmeal

6 Muscovy duck breasts, deboned with skin on
Salt and freshly ground black pepper

 **For the sauce:** In a small bowl, combine cherries and port. Cover and chill overnight.

In a saucepan, combine cherry mixture, water, chicken stock, vinegar, butter, and shallots. Cover and simmer over low heat until cherries have absorbed most of the liquid. Place mixture in the bowl of a food processor and process until smooth. In a saucepan, add the cream and reduce by half over medium-low heat. Stir in the cherry mixture and simmer over low heat until sauce is slightly thickened. Season to taste with salt and pepper.

For the garlic purée: Preheat oven to 250° F. Remove the papery outer skins from the garlic, leaving whole heads intact. Slice $^1/4$ inch off the top. Place in a small baking dish and drizzle with butter and olive oil. Season with salt and pepper. Bake for about 2 hours, basting occasionally, until garlic is very tender. Remove from oven and cool. Squeeze garlic from skins into the butter and oil mixture. Mash until smooth.

For the polenta: In a large heavy saucepan, combine chicken stock, cream, water, garlic purée, and salt. Bring to a boil over medium-high heat. Whisking constantly, slowly add the cornmeal in a thin stream. Continue whisking until mixture is slightly thickened and creamy.

Prepare the grill. Season the duck breasts with salt and pepper. Place duck skin-side-down on the grill. Cook for about 10 minutes on each side. To serve, ladle polenta onto a plate. Slice the duck breast across the grain and arrange the meat in a fan shape on top of the polenta. Ladle sauce over duck and serve.

Serves 6
Serve with Markham Vineyards
Merlot

BELVEDERE VINEYARDS
AND WINERY

In Italian, Belvedere means "beautiful view," which aptly describes the vista from this rustic redwood winery in the Russian River Valley. The winery was built in 1982, the same year owners Bill and Sally Hambrecht bought their first piece of vineyard land high atop Bradford Mountain in Dry Creek Valley. Over the years they purchased and planted additional estate vineyards in the Dry Creek, Alexander, and Russian River Valleys in northern Sonoma County. As Bill Hambrecht often says, "Our most valuable asset is our vineyards. Good vineyards are as valuable as gold to a winery, and Belvedere has access to some of Sonoma County's best."

ANEC AMB FIGUES
(Duck with Figs)

Chef Antonio Buenvia of San Francisco's
Vinga Restaurant has recreated a
traditional, hearty autumn recipe from
his native Catalan region of Spain.

2 cups sweet vermouth

18 dried figs, cut in half

2 tablespoons olive oil

8 duck legs

Salt and freshly ground black pepper

4 cups chicken stock

2 cups veal or duck stock

8 small potatoes, peeled and boiled
    until tender

12 fresh figs

In a bowl, combine vermouth and dried figs and let marinate overnight.

In a large skillet, heat olive oil over medium-high heat. Place duck legs, skin-side-down, in hot pan. Sear until well browned on both sides. Remove duck from skillet and pour off fat. Return duck to skillet and season with salt and pepper. Add the vermouth and figs and simmer until liquid is reduced by half. Add the chicken stock and veal

(recipe continued on next page)

stock and bring to a boil. Reduce heat to medium-low, cover, and simmer for about 1 hour.

Remove the duck to a platter and keep warm. Skim off fat. Place liquid and figs in the bowl of a food processor and process until smooth. Serve 2 duck legs per person, and pour some of the sauce over the top. Serve 2 potatoes per person and garnish with 3 fresh figs.

Serves 4
Serve with Belvedere Vineyards and Winery
Merlot

To be crushed
in the winepress of passion.
Gabriel Biel

1996

TURNBULL

Cabernet
Sauvignon

Napa Valley
Oakville

Produced & Bottled by
Turnbull Wine Cellars   Oakville, CA

TURNBULL WINE CELLARS

Just south of Oakville in the Napa Valley, Patrick O'Dell, proprietor of Turnbull Wine Cellars, produces stunning wines of amazing complexity and depth. His well-known red wines include Cabernet Sauvignon, Merlot, and Sangiovese, as well as small amounts of Syrah and Zinfandel. A limited amount of elegant Sauvignon Blanc is a special treat for white-wine lovers who visit his tasting room.

SIMPLY CASSOULET

Beverley Wolfe has developed a simplified version of cassoulet that allows the cook to spend plenty of time with her guests before dinner.

1 pound dried lima beans or other dried white beans, soaked overnight in cold water

4 ounces bacon, diced

1 onion, chopped

1 cup diced carrots

1 cup diced celery

$1/2$ cup chopped Italian parsley

15 cloves garlic, minced

$1/2$ cup chopped sundried tomatoes

2 tablespoons minced fresh thyme

2 bay leaves

1 duck, cut into 8 pieces (the legs and breasts cut in half)

4 lamb shanks

$1/4$ cup brandy

1 pound garlic sausages

$1^1/2$ cups Turnbull Wine Cellars Chardonnay

4 to 6 cups duck stock or chicken stock

1 teaspoon salt

1 teaspoon freshly ground black pepper

3 cups Italian breadcrumbs

Preheat oven to 325° F.

In a large skillet, cook the bacon over medium heat until crisp. Drain bacon on paper towels then put in the bottom of a large ovenproof pot. Discard all but 1 tablespoon of the fat in the skillet. Place onion, carrots, celery, and parsley in skillet and sauté until onion is translucent. Add garlic and sauté until fragrant. Add vegetables to the bacon in the pot. Add sundried tomatoes, thyme, and bay leaves to the pot. Add the duck, skin-side-down, to the skillet and brown well. Turn and brown on the other side. Place duck on top of the vegetable mixture. Discard all but 1 tablespoon of the fat in the skillet. Add the lamb to the skillet and brown well on all sides. Add lamb to pot and discard excess fat in skillet. Return skillet to stove and whisk in brandy, scraping up any browned bits. Pour into pot. Add sausages and wine to pot. Drain beans and add them to the pot. Add enough stock to just cover the beans. Add salt and pepper. Cover the pot and place in oven for about 4 hours. Check the cassoulet every hour, adding more stock if it gets too dry.

After 3½ hours, remove pot from oven and skim off fat. Sprinkle breadcrumbs over the top of the cassoulet. Return pot to oven, uncovered, for the remaining 30 minutes to toast the breadcrumbs. Serve in warmed shallow bowls.

Serves 8
Serve with Turnbull Wine Cellars
Cabernet Sauvignon

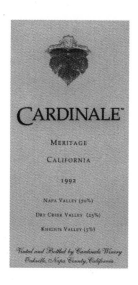

CARDINALE

Cardinale Rule: Make grape selection an obsession and gentle winemaking a virtue. Grow fruit of intense vineyard and varietal character from the finest sites in the Mayacamas. Pick only when the fruit is physiologically ripe and balanced in flavor. Hand harvest into small lug boxes, during the cool of the morning. Keep each vineyard separate, in order to know it better. Hand sort all fruit and use only sound, ripe berries. Carefully crack the berries and begin native yeast fermentation. Let juice and skins macerate gently for twenty-five to thirty-five days to maximize flavor and texture. Use a traditional basket press to deepen mid-palate flavors. Place into 100 percent new tight-grained French oak château barrels. Attentively rack wine from barrel to barrel every three months. Age in barrel for eighteen to twenty-one months. Bottle unfiltered. Age in bottle for twelve months before release. Enjoy or bottle age for an additional five to ten years.

OVEN-BRAISED SHORT RIBS

This rich and hearty dish is delicious served with soft polenta.

6 pounds beef short ribs with bones

Salt and freshly ground black pepper

Flour for dredging

1/4 cup olive oil

2 onions, chopped

2 carrots, peeled and sliced

2 stalks celery, sliced

2 parsnips, peeled and sliced

1 tomato, chopped

2 cloves garlic, minced

2 cups Cardinale Meritage

2 cups beef stock

1 tablespoon minced fresh oregano

1 tablespoon minced Italian parsley

1 tablespoon minced fresh thyme

1 teaspoon minced orange zest

(recipe continued on next page)

🍂 Preheat oven to 350° F. Lightly oil a roasting pan with a tightly fitting lid, large enough to hold the short ribs in one layer.

Season the short ribs well with salt and pepper. Dredge in flour and shake off the excess. In a large skillet, heat the olive oil over medium-high heat. Brown the short ribs well on all sides. Place in one layer in the prepared roasting pan.

In the same skillet, sauté the onions, carrots, celery, parsnips, tomato, and garlic over medium heat until barely tender. Pour vegetables over meat. Whisk the wine into the skillet, scraping up any browned bits. Pour wine into the roasting pan. Stir together beef stock, oregano, parsley, thyme, and orange zest and pour mixture over ribs. Cover tightly and place in oven. Cook for 2½ to 3 hours, basting several times, until meat is very tender and sauce is thick.

Serves 6 to 8
Serve with Cardinale Meritage

TREFETHEN VINEYARDS

Tradition combines with technology at Trefethen Vineyards, where a century-old winery and the latest in winemaking equipment give the Trefethen family, and their wines, the best of both worlds. First planted with grapes in the 1850s, the Eshcol ranch, as it was known back then, received its name from a biblical allusion to an immense cluster of grapes. In 1968, Gene and Katie Trefethen revitalized the old Eshcol property and planted new vines on the 600-acre valley estate and on fifty acres to the northwest. The first wines were vinified in 1973, and today wine production has climbed to 75,000 cases per year. The Trefethen family has this to say about their wines: "Winemaking is part agriculture and part parenting. We are proud to introduce you to what we have worried over and cared for—our wines. They are meant to be shared and enjoyed among friends."

BLACK PEPPER–RUBBED SIRLOIN
with Red Onion & Cabernet Relish

The robust flavors of this dish would be best framed by a side of creamy garlic mashed potatoes.

**RED ONION
AND CABERNET RELISH:**

2 cups Trefethen Vineyards Cabernet Sauvignon

2 red onions, chopped

1 cup sugar

1/2 cup red wine vinegar

1 tablespoon minced fresh thyme

1 tablespoon pickling spice, tied in cheesecloth

1 bay leaf

6 (8-ounce) sirloin steaks

3 cloves garlic, minced

3 tablespoons cracked black pepper

2 tablespoons salt

Olive oil for searing the steaks

🍂 **For the relish:** In a heavy saucepan, stir together wine, onions, sugar, vinegar, thyme, pickling spice, and bay leaf. Bring to a boil over medium-high heat. Reduce heat to medium and simmer until mixture is reduced to a thick relish. Stir often to prevent scorching. Remove pickling spice and bay leaf and discard. Pour relish into a small serving bowl.

For the steaks: Rub steaks all over with garlic. Stir together salt and pepper in a shallow dish. Press steaks into mixture, coating both sides. Let sit for 20 minutes.

Heat a large cast-iron skillet over medium-high heat. Add enough oil to coat the bottom of the skillet. When almost smoking, add steaks in one layer. Sear well on both sides until crispy, browned, and medium-rare. Serve topped with relish.

Serves 6
Serve with Trefethen Vineyards
Cabernet Sauvignon

CABERNET SAUVIGNON
SONOMA COUNTY

ALC. 13.3% BY VOL.

GEYSER PEAK
WINERY

*Located just north of Healdsburg, 100-year-old
Geyser Peak Winery's tradition of excellence
shows in their being named "1998 Winery of the
Year" by* Wine & Spirits *magazine and the
San Francisco International Wine Competition. Their original vine-covered stone winery
is now the cornerstone of a state-of-the-art complex that is one of the most well-equipped
wineries in California. Within the winery, pres-
ident and head winemaker Daryl Groom over-
sees the vinification of not only their sought-
after reserve wines, but also a multitude of
great wines for all occasions.*

GRILLED RIB EYE STEAKS *with Horseradish Butter & Caramelized-Onion Mashed Potatoes*

The sweetness of the caramelized-onion mashed potatoes beautifully complements the spicy horseradish butter.

HORSERADISH BUTTER:

4 tablespoons butter, softened

2 tablespoons prepared horseradish

$1/2$ teaspoon salt

CARAMELIZED-ONION MASHED POTATOES:

2 tablespoons butter

3 onions, chopped

1 teaspoon sugar

2 tablespoons water

4 potatoes, peeled and quartered

$1/4$ cup sour cream

2 tablespoons butter

1 teaspoon salt

1 teaspoon freshly ground black pepper

6 (5 ounce) rib eye steaks

Salt and freshly ground black pepper

(recipe continued on next page)

For the horseradish butter: In a small bowl, combine butter, horseradish, and salt. Mash together with the back of a fork until well blended. Place mixture on a piece of plastic wrap and form into a log about 3 inches long. Chill at least 1 hour or until firm. Cut into 6 slices and keep chilled.

For the potatoes: In a large skillet, melt the butter over medium heat. Add the onions, sugar, and water and sauté until tender. Cover tightly and reduce heat to medium-low. Simmer for about 45 minutes to 1 hour, stirring every 10 minutes and adding a little more water if necessary so onions do not burn, until onions are deep golden brown. Bring a large pot of water to a boil. Add potatoes and cook until very tender. Drain well and return potatoes to pot. Add caramelized onions, sour cream, butter, salt, and pepper and mash together until blended. Keep warm.

For the steaks: Prepare the grill. Season steaks with salt and pepper and grill over a hot fire for 4 to 6 minutes per side (for medium-rare). Divide potatoes onto 6 plates, top with a steak and a slice of horseradish butter.

Serves 6
Serve with Geyser Peak Winery
Cabernet Sauvignon

DRY CREEK VINEYARD

Dry Creek Vineyard was the first new winery to be established in the Dry Creek Valley of Sonoma after Prohibition. Synonymous with fine winemaking, Dry Creek Vineyard draws upon over thirty-five different vineyards to produce their wines, matching the particular soils and microclimates of each site to the varieties that do best.

"ZINFUL" FLANK STEAK

This intensely flavorful recipe tastes as good off the grill in the heat of summer as it does oven-broiled in the middle of winter.

1 (2-pound) flank steak

MARINADE:

3/4 cup balsamic vinegar

1/4 cup olive oil

3 cloves garlic, minced

2 teaspoons basil

2 teaspoons oregano

2 teaspoons thyme

1/2 teaspoon salt

1/2 teaspoon freshly ground black pepper

ZINFANDEL SAUCE:

1 small onion, chopped

1 shallot, chopped

1 clove garlic, minced

2 cups Dry Creek Vineyard Zinfandel

🍃 With a sharp knife, lightly score the flank steak with a diamond pattern on both sides.

For the marinade: In a shallow dish, whisk together the vinegar, oil, garlic, basil, oregano, thyme, salt, and pepper. Place the steak in the marinade, cover, and refrigerate overnight.

For the sauce: In the bowl of a food processor, combine the onion, shallot, and garlic and process until smooth. In a saucepan, combine the onion mixture with the Zinfandel and bring to a boil. Reduce heat to low and simmer until mixture is reduced by half. Remove flank steak from marinade and pour marinade into saucepan. Bring to a boil, then reduce heat to low and simmer for 5 minutes.

Grill or broil flank steak about 5 minutes per side (for medium-rare). Slice thinly across the grain and serve with the Zinfandel sauce.

Serves 6
Serve with Dry Creek Vineyard
Zinfandel

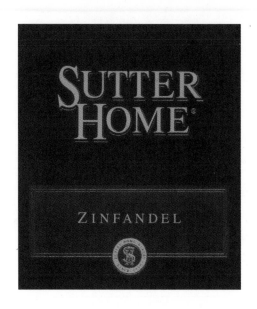

SUTTER HOME
WINERY

Sutter Home is one of California's enviable success stories. Begun in 1874, the winery passed into the hands of its current family-owners in 1947 when John and Mario Trinchero immigrated from Italy and set down roots in the Napa Valley. Today their children carry on this once mom-and-pop operation. A milestone occurred in 1972 when, in an effort to make his red Zinfandel more robust, Bob Trinchero drew off some of the free run juice and fermented it as a "white" wine. This pale pink wine became a favorite at the winery's tasting room, and thus was born White Zinfandel. Today Sutter Home is known not only for this invention, but also for their high-quality, affordable varietal wines and their line of nonalcoholic wines.

PRIME RIB ROAST
with 30 Cloves of Garlic & Zinfandel Sauce

The half-hour rest after removing the roast from the oven is essential. The interior of the roast will continue to increase in temperature while the juices become locked into the meat. Enjoy this hearty dish, from chef Jeffry Starr, on a cold wintry day.

1 (4-pound) cross rib roast

10 cloves garlic, sliced in half lengthwise

Salt and freshly ground black pepper

ZINFANDEL SAUCE:

20 cloves garlic

1 tablespoon olive oil

3/4 cup Sutter Home Winery Zinfandel

2 tablespoons finely chopped shallots

1 tablespoon minced fresh thyme

2 tablespoons butter

Salt and freshly ground black pepper

(recipe continued on next page)

❧ Preheat oven to 500° F. Lightly oil a roasting pan. Place roast in prepared roasting pan. With a sharp paring knife, make 1 to 2-inch slits in the meat and insert sliced garlic slivers. Season well with salt and pepper. Roast for 15 minutes, then reduce oven to 325° F. Continue to roast for about 18 minutes per pound for medium-rare, or until internal temperature reaches 125° F. Remove meat to a cutting board, cover with foil, and let rest for 30 minutes before carving to retain juices.

For the sauce: Toss garlic and olive oil together. Wrap in foil and cook in oven during the last 45 minutes of roasting meat. Place garlic cloves in a small bowl and mash until smooth.

After removing meat from roasting pan, place pan on top of stove over medium-high heat. Skim off excess fat from pan. Whisk in the wine, scraping up any browned bits. Add reserved garlic, shallots, and thyme and simmer until slightly thickened. Whisk in butter and season with salt and pepper. Transfer to a sauceboat.

Serves 6
Serve with Sutter Home Winery
Zinfandel

RODNEY STRONG
VINEYARDS

Over thirty-five years ago, Rodney Strong was one of the first to recognize Sonoma County's potential for excellence. After searching for vineyard land that would bring each grape variety to its fullest potential, Rodney Strong finally selected vineyard sites in the Chalk Hill, Alexander Valley, and Russian River Valley appellations to produce his wine. In the cellar, he employs the subtle use of barrel and stainless steel fermentation, oak aging, and other winemaking techniques to bring out the best in the fruit. All this is in keeping with his philosophy to allow the grapes from each vineyard to express their individual character in the final bottled wine.

FRENCH LAMB SHANK STEW

3 tablespoons olive oil

6 lamb shanks

3 leeks, white and pale green part only, chopped

1 onion, chopped

4 cloves garlic, chopped

1/4 cup finely chopped fresh parsley

1 tablespoon minced fresh rosemary

2 (14-ounce) cans chicken stock

2 (15-ounce) cans white beans, drained

1 teaspoon salt

1 teaspoon freshly ground black pepper

1 bay leaf

In a heavy Dutch oven with a tightly fitting lid, heat olive oil over medium heat. Add the lamb shanks and brown well on all sides. Remove lamb and add leeks, onion, garlic, parsley, and rosemary. Sauté until tender. Whisk in chicken stock, scraping up any browned bits. Stir in beans, salt, pepper, and bay leaf. Return lamb to pot and cover tightly. Reduce heat to medium low and cook for 2 1/2 hours.

Halfway through cooking time, turn the lamb shanks over. If stew is too liquid, remove lid and simmer until slightly thickened.

Serves 6
Serve with Rodney Strong Vineyards
Pinot Noir

Forsake not an old friend; for the new is not comparable to him: a new friend is as new wine; when it is old, it is drunk with pleasure.

The Bible

NAVARRO VINEYARDS

There are few wineries in northern California that have had the success with their wines that Navarro Vineyards has experienced. Visitors to this winery's tasting room, when asking about one of the current vintages, are often sorrowfully informed, "Sorry, the Chardonnay and Pinot Noir have sold out." This speaks to the absolute quality standards that Ted Bennet and Deborah Cahn have set for the wines they make. Known for their incredible delicacy and fruit, Navarro's wines are not just your standard California varietals. In addition to their outstanding Pinot Noir and Chardonnay, they take great pains to keep other, lesser-known wines in production. Their Chenin Blanc, White Riesling, and Gewürztraminers are known to wine lovers as among the world's finest, and their Sauvignon Blanc, Pinot Gris, Muscat Blanc, and Valdiguié never fail to charm first-time tasters.

MOROCCAN KEFTA
with Jeweled Rice

*Aromas of the Casbah will swirl through
your house when you serve this intriguing
and mouth-watering Moroccan favorite.*

MOROCCAN KEFTA:

2 pounds ground lamb

1 small onion, grated

$1/3$ cup finely chopped cilantro

2 cloves garlic, finely minced

1 teaspoon oregano

$1/2$ teaspoon cumin

$1/2$ teaspoon freshly ground black pepper

$1/2$ teaspoon paprika

$1/2$ teaspoon salt

$1/8$ teaspoon cayenne

JEWELED RICE:

$1/4$ cup olive oil

$1 1/2$ cups rice

$1/2$ cup finely chopped onion

2 cloves garlic, minced

$1/2$ teaspoon turmeric

3 cups chicken stock

$1/3$ cup golden raisins

1 teaspoon salt

$1/3$ cup almonds, lightly toasted and chopped

$1/4$ cup finely chopped fresh parsley

(recipe continued on next page)

For the kefta: In a large bowl, combine lamb, onion, cilantro, garlic, oregano, cumin, pepper, paprika, salt, and cayenne and knead together for 5 minutes. Cover and chill 1 hour to allow flavors to marry.

For the rice: In a saucepan, heat the oil over medium-high heat. Add the rice and stir until rice starts to turn golden. Add the onion and garlic and sauté until fragrant. Stir in the turmeric. Stir in the chicken stock, raisins, and salt and bring to a boil. Reduce heat to low, cover, and simmer for about 20 minutes, or until rice is tender and all liquid is absorbed. Stir in the almonds and parsley.

Preheat broiler. Lightly oil a broiling pan. Form lamb mixture into 12 sausage shapes and place on prepared pan. Broil about 5 minutes per side or until done. Serve on top of the rice.

Serves 6
Serve with Navarro Vineyards
Pinot Noir Methode a l'ancienne

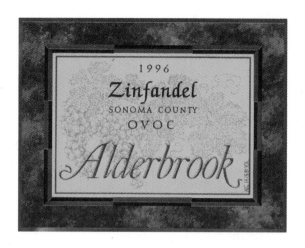

ALDERBROOK VINEYARDS
AND WINERY

*The Dry Creek Valley, just to the west of Healds-
burg, is home to Alderbrook Vineyards and Winery. Purchased by George Gillemot in 1991, Alderbrook has been on an upward course ever since.
Chardonnay, Sauvignon Blanc, Gewürztraminer,
Zinfandel, Pinot Noir, Syrah, Merlot, Cabernet
Sauvignon, and Viognier are among the wines produced by this medal-winning winery. The quality of
Alderbrook's wines can be directly traced to their
stated goal: "To produce the very finest wines of the
Dry Creek Valley."*

SUMMER LAMB RAGOUT *with Sundried Tomatoes & Peppers*

Serve over polenta or alongside pasta tossed with fresh basil.

1/2 cup all-purpose flour

2 teaspoons salt, divided

1 1/2 teaspoons freshly ground black pepper, divided

1 pound lamb shoulder or leg, cut into
    1/2-inch cubes

1/4 cup olive oil

1 onion, chopped

2 cloves garlic, minced

3/4 cup Alderbrook Winery Zinfandel

3/4 cup water

12 dried tomato halves, sliced

1 tablespoon minced fresh thyme

1 green bell pepper, cut into strips

1 red bell pepper, cut into strips

1 yellow bell pepper, cut into strips

1 Anaheim chile, seeded and diced

1 eggplant, cut into 1-inch cubes

1 potato, peeled and diced

1 zucchini, cut into cubes

🍂 Preheat oven to 350°F.

In a shallow dish, stir together flour, 1 teaspoon of the salt, and $^1/2$ teaspoon of the pepper. Dredge lamb in flour mixture, coating all sides. In a large ovenproof pot with a tightly fitting lid, heat olive oil over medium heat. Add lamb and brown well on all sides. Add onion and garlic and sauté 5 minutes. Stir in wine, water, tomatoes, and thyme and simmer 5 minutes. Add bell peppers, chile, eggplant, potato, zucchini, 1 teaspoon salt, and 1 teaspoon pepper and stir well. Cover, place in the oven, and braise for about 1 hour and 30 minutes, or until lamb is very tender and sauce has thickened.

Serves 6
Serve with Alderbrook Winery
Zinfandel

OAKVILLE RANCH
VINEYARDS AND WINERY

Located on the Silverado Trail in a new and modern winery, Oakville Ranch Vineyards and Winery produces inky, dark Cabernets and Merlots, as well as complex and balanced Chardonnays from their estate vineyards high up in the eastern hills of the Oakville appellation of the Napa Valley. Low yields from the ancient, rocky volcanic soil serve to amplify and intensify the structure of these classic Napa Valley wines. Additionally, small lots of Sauvignon Blanc, Viognier, Pinot Noir, Zinfandel, Syrah, and Sangiovese are available in limited quantities.

BRAISED
LAMB SHANKS

This meltingly tender rendition of braised shanks has just the proper balance of flavor to bring out the fruit of Cabernet Sauvignon.

4 lamb shanks

Salt and freshly ground black pepper

3 tablespoons olive oil

1 onion, chopped

2 carrots, peeled and diced

1 stalk celery, diced

4 cloves garlic, minced

3 tablespoons tomato paste

1/2 cup Oakville Ranch Winery
   Cabernet Sauvignon

4 cups beef stock

2 dried mission figs, diced

5 whole cloves

1 stick cinnamon

(recipe continued on next page)

🐿 Season lamb with salt and pepper. In a large Dutch oven, heat olive oil over medium heat. Add lamb shanks and brown well on all sides. Remove lamb to a platter. Pour off excess fat from the Dutch oven and return to the stove. Add onion, carrots, and celery and sauté until very tender and beginning to brown. Add garlic and sauté until fragrant. Stir in tomato paste and sauté until mixture begins to turn brown. Whisk in wine and simmer until reduced by half. Stir in beef stock and simmer until reduced by half. Return lamb shanks to pot, reduce heat to medium-low, cover, and simmer for 30 minutes. Turn lamb shanks over and add figs, cloves, and cinnamon stick. Cover and simmer an additional 30 to 45 minutes, or until very tender.

Remove lamb to a platter and keep warm. Strain sauce through a sieve and discard the solids. Return liquid to pot and reduce, over medium heat, until sauce is thick. Pour sauce over lamb. Serve with mashed parsnips.

Serves 4
Serve with Oakville Ranch Winery
Cabernet Sauvignon

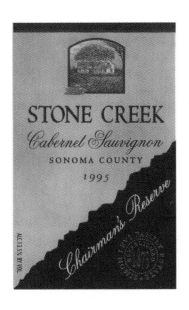

STONE CREEK
WINERY

Stone Creek's Tasting Room is located in Kenwood in the heart of Sonoma County, in what was once a one-room schoolhouse. This historical building was erected in 1890, and was one of the first public schools in the Los Guilicos Valley. In addition to its colorful history, the "Old Blue Schoolhouse" is now the happy home of Stone Creek Wines.

OSSO BUCCO *with*
Rosemary-Cabernet Sauce

*Chef Marc Downie of Catering by Design
came up with this variation on a northern
Italian favorite. Roasted potatoes would be
an excellent accompaniment.*

6 veal shanks

Salt and freshly ground black pepper

$1/2$ cup all-purpose flour

2 tablespoons olive oil

2 cloves garlic, minced

$1/2$ cup sliced mushrooms

$1/3$ cup fresh rosemary, chopped

About 3 cups Stone Creek Winery
    Cabernet Sauvignon

1 teaspoon butter

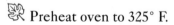 Preheat oven to 325° F.

Season the veal shanks with salt and pepper.
Place flour in a shallow dish. Dredge veal in flour
and shake off the excess. In a large skillet, heat
olive oil over medium heat. Add the garlic and
sauté until just fragrant. Add the veal and brown
well on both sides. Transfer veal to a roasting pan

just large enough to hold the veal in one layer. Top with mushrooms and rosemary. Pour in enough wine to just cover the veal. Cover roasting pan and place in oven. Roast for 2 to 2^1/2 hours, or until meat is very tender.

Remove from oven and place veal and mushrooms on a serving platter. Place roasting pan on top of the stove over medium heat. Whisk up any browned bits and reduce liquid until thickened to a sauce consistency. Strain liquid and discard solids. Whisk in butter. Pour sauce over veal and serve.

Serves 6
Serve with Stone Creek Winery Chairman's
Reserve North Coast Cabernet Sauvignon

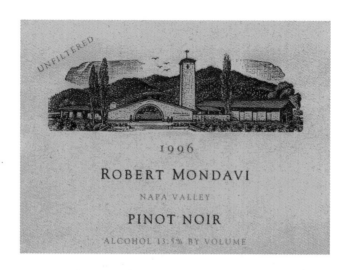

UNFILTERED

1996

ROBERT MONDAVI

NAPA VALLEY

PINOT NOIR

ALCOHOL 13.5% BY VOLUME

ROBERT MONDAVI WINERY

Founded in 1966 by Robert Mondavi and his son, Michael, the Robert Mondavi Winery is considered a leader in the modern wine industry. They are committed to producing naturally balanced wines of great finesse and elegance that complement and enhance fine food. They have been successful in achieving these goals through earth-friendly farming practices, a sophisticated winery emphasizing gentle treatment of their wines, and a genuine love for their handiwork. No other winery epitomizes the Napa Valley like the Robert Mondavi Winery.

TAPENADE-CRUSTED RACK OF LAMB
with Pinot Noir Sauce

Mediterranean flavors and aromas from this robust dish, created by chef Sarah Scott, call to mind a simpler way of living. Good friends, great food, and fine wine…what better way to spend a lazy Sunday afternoon?

TAPENADE:

1 cup pitted Kalamata olives

1 tablespoon capers

1 tablespoon minced garlic

1 tablespoon freshly squeezed lemon juice

2 anchovies, rinsed and patted dry

Zest of 1 lemon

$1/2$ teaspoon freshly ground black pepper

$1/4$ cup olive oil

2 racks of lamb with 8 ribs

3 tablespoons olive oil

1 cup tapenade

3 cups panko bread crumbs

(recipe continued on next page)

PINOT NOIR SAUCE:

1 tablespoon olive oil

4 shallots, minced

3 cloves garlic, minced

6 ounces mushrooms, sliced

2 tablespoons minced fresh Italian parsley

1 teaspoon minced fresh thyme

1 bay leaf

2 cups Robert Mondavi Winery Pinot Noir

2 cups lamb or beef stock

Salt and freshly ground black pepper

For the tapenade: In the bowl of a food processor, combine olives, capers, garlic, lemon juice, anchovies, lemon zest, and pepper and process until smooth, scraping sides of the bowl often. With the motor running, add the olive oil in a thin stream until all is incorporated and mixture is smooth. Set aside.

For the lamb: Preheat oven to 375° F. Lightly oil a roasting pan.

In a large skillet, heat the olive oil over medium-high heat. Sear the fat-side of the lamb well. Remove the racks and blot off excess oil with a paper towel. Spread the tapenade over the fat-side of the lamb. Press the bread crumbs onto the tapenade. Place the lamb, fat-side-up, in the prepared roasting pan. Roast for about 25 to 30 minutes for medium-rare, or until internal temperature reaches 130° F. Remove meat to a cutting board and let rest for 5 minutes before carving.

For the sauce: In a saucepan, heat olive oil over medium heat. Add the shallots and garlic and sauté until fragrant. Add the mushrooms and sauté until tender. Add the parsley, thyme, and bay leaf. Stir in the wine and simmer until reduced by half. Add the stock and reduce again by half. Season with salt and pepper.

Carve lamb into double chops and serve with the sauce.

Serves 6 to 8
Serve with Robert Mondavi Winery
Pinot Noir

HESS COLLECTION WINERY

The Hess Collection embraces both art and wine passionately. Their commitment to quality is evident in the contemporary paintings and sculpture lining the galleries of the Visitor Center. It is also evident inside each bottle of their wine—from the acclaimed Hess Collection label to the popular Hess Select wines. Born of a desire to offer distinctive products at reasonable prices, The Hess Collection has embarked on a global journey. The Hess Collection New World Wines has formed partnerships with family-owned producers from Chile, South Africa, Argentina, and Italy who share the common thread of commitment to excellence.

ROASTED RACK OF VEAL
with Mustard & Herbs

When the occasion calls for a rich and satisfying splurge, turn to this grand and glorious centerpiece from Katie Sutton.

VEGETABLE MÉLANGE:

12 small red-skinned potatoes, quartered

2 heads garlic, papery skin removed and
   1/4 inch of the top sliced off

1/4 cup olive oil

Salt and freshly ground black pepper

12 spears asparagus, cut into thirds

12 pearl onions

3 tablespoons butter, divided

2 teaspoons sugar

1 1/2 cups sliced chanterelle mushrooms

1 1/2 cups sliced portobello mushrooms

1 1/2 cups sliced shiitake mushrooms,
   stems discarded

(recipe continued on next page)

ROASTED RACK OF VEAL:

1 1/2 cups plain breadcrumbs

1/2 cup minced fresh parsley

1 tablespoon minced fresh tarragon

1 tablespoon minced fresh thyme

1 teaspoon minced fresh oregano

3/4 cup butter, melted

3 tablespoons olive oil

1 rack of veal with 6 bones

Salt and freshly ground black pepper

3/4 cup Dijon mustard

CABERNET SAUCE:

1/4 cup butter

6 shallots, minced

1 cup Hess Collection Winery Cabernet Sauvignon

3 cups veal stock

5 tablespoons Dijon mustard

5 tablespoons chopped fresh parsley

Salt and freshly ground black pepper

Preheat oven to 425° F. Lightly oil a roasting pan. Put potatoes and garlic into prepared roasting pan. Drizzle olive oil over and season with salt and pepper. Roast until potatoes are tender, about 20 minutes. Remove potatoes and set aside. Return garlic to oven and roast an additional 20 minutes, or until garlic is very tender. Remove from oven and squeeze garlic from the skins. Set aside.

Bring a pot of water to a boil over high heat. Blanch asparagus for 45 seconds. Drain, then plunge into an ice water bath to refresh asparagus. Set aside.

In a small saucepan, combine pearl onions, 1 tablespoon of the butter, sugar, and enough water to come halfway over the onions. Cover and simmer over medium heat for about 10 minutes, or until tender. Set aside.

In a large skillet, melt remaining 2 tablespoons butter over medium-high heat. Add the mushrooms and sauté until tender. Set aside.

For the veal: In a bowl, stir together breadcrumbs, parsley, tarragon, thyme, and oregano until well mixed. Stir in melted butter until evenly moistened. Set aside.

In a very large skillet, heat the olive oil over high heat. Sear the veal all over until golden. Remove the veal and blot off excess oil with paper towel. Place veal in a roasting pan. Season well with salt and pepper. Spread mustard over veal. Press the reserved breadcrumb mixture onto mustard. Roast until internal temperature reaches 130° F. Remove veal to a cutting board and let rest for 30 minutes before carving.

For the sauce: Place the roasting pan with the drippings from the veal on top of the stove over medium heat. Add the butter and shallots and sauté until tender. Add the wine and simmer until reduced by half. Whisk in the veal stock and mustard and simmer until reduced by half again. Strain and discard solids. Stir in parsley and season with salt and pepper.

To serve: In a large skillet, combine reserved potatoes, roasted garlic, asparagus, pearl onions, and mushrooms. Sauté over medium heat until hot. Divide onto six plates. Carve the rack of veal between each bone and place 1 chop next to the vegetables. Spoon sauce over the top.

Serves 6
Serve with Hess Collection Winery
Cabernet Sauvignon

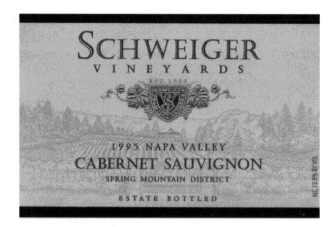

SCHWEIGER VINEYARDS
AND WINERY

Fred and Sally Schweiger have turned their estate winery into one of the most picturesque properties in the Napa Valley. Located high above St. Helena, atop Spring Mountain, their vines have found ideal growing conditions within the volcanic ash soils of this section of the Mayacamas mountain range. Chardonnay, Merlot, and Cabernet Sauvignon are the three varieties upon which the Schweigers have built their reputation. Opulent with fruit, the red wines exhibit firm tannins and fine structure, while their Chardonnay astounds with supple mouth-filling elegance.

GRILLED PORK TENDERLOIN *with* *Cabernet Cumberland Sauce*

Glossy and burgundy-colored, this sweet-and-sour sauce turns tender pork medallions into an elegant entrée.

CABERNET CUMBERLAND SAUCE:

1 cup Schweiger Vineyards Cabernet Sauvignon

1/3 cup beef stock

2 tablespoons minced shallots

2 teaspoons minced dried cherries

1/8 teaspoon ground cloves

1/8 teaspoon thyme

2 tablespoons red currant jelly

2 teaspoons brown sugar

$1^1/2$ teaspoons freshly squeezed lemon juice

$1^1/2$ teaspoons Dijon mustard

$1^1/2$ teaspoons cornstarch

2 tablespoons cold water

Salt and freshly ground black pepper

$1^1/2$ to 2 pounds pork tenderloin

Salt and freshly ground black pepper

(recipe continued on next page)

For the sauce: In a saucepan, combine wine, beef stock, shallots, cherries, cloves, and thyme. Bring to a boil over medium heat and simmer until mixture is reduced by one-third. Strain and discard solids. Return wine mixture to saucepan and whisk in currant jelly, brown sugar, lemon juice, and mustard. In a small bowl, stir together cornstarch and cold water until smooth. Whisk cornstarch mixture into sauce. Simmer over medium heat until thickened. Season with salt and pepper. Keep warm over low heat.

For the pork: Prepare the grill. Season pork well with salt and pepper. Place on hot grill and cook on all sides until internal temperature reaches 140° F. Remove from grill and let rest 10 minutes before carving. Carve into 6 medallions and serve on top of a pool of sauce.

Serves 6
Serve with Schweiger Vineyards
Cabernet Sauvignon

KENDALL-JACKSON
WINERY

In 1974, Jess Jackson and his family purchased an 85-acre pear ranch near Lakeport in northern California. By 1982, the ranch was a vineyard, the barn was a tasting room, and the pasture was a winery. Meanwhile, they studied the premium vineyards that span California's cool coastal growing regions and discovered the wonderful spectrum of flavors produced by the same grape varietal grown in different locations. Why not use this exciting diversity? Why not blend the best grapes from the best vineyards to produce unique wines with layers of depth and complexity? Their first Chardonnay was made in 1982, from vineyards in Santa Barbara, Monterey, Sonoma, and Lake Counties. This wine was named "Best American Chardonnay" by the American Wine Competition. Their concept of blending the best with the best was affirmed and to this day continues to be the reason their wines are noted for their consistency and complexity, vintage after vintage.

SPICED PORK TENDERLOIN
with Chardonnay Glaze

Tess McDonough and Ed Walsh use the technique of soaking the pork in brine overnight, which keeps the meat incredibly moist and juicy.

2 pork tenderloins, about 1 pound each

BRINE:

2 quarts ice water

1/4 cup kosher salt

1 onion, sliced

1 bunch parsley, chopped

3 bay leaves

5 juniper berries, crushed

5 black peppercorns, crushed

SPICE RUB:

2 teaspoons whole coriander seed

2 teaspoons whole fennel seed

2 teaspoons whole mustard seed

Salt and freshly ground black pepper

1/4 cup olive oil

2 cups Kendall-Jackson Chardonnay

For the brine: In a large nonaluminum bowl, whisk ice water and salt together until salt dissolves. Stir in onion, parsley, bay leaves, juniper berries, and peppercorns. Place pork in brine. Place a small plate on top of pork to keep it submerged. Cover and refrigerate overnight.

For the spice rub: In a small sauté pan, toast the coriander, fennel, and mustard seeds over medium-high heat, just until they start to pop. Place the spices in a mortar and pestle and crush.

Remove pork from brine, rinse well, then pat dry. Sprinkle pork with salt and pepper. Rub spice mixture into pork, coating all sides. In a sauté pan, heat the olive oil over medium-high heat. Add the pork and brown well on all sides. Reduce heat to medium-low and continue cooking until meat thermometer inserted in the thickest part registers 155° F. Remove pork and let rest on a platter for 10 minutes before carving. Increase heat to medium-high and whisk wine into sauté pan, scraping up any browned bits. Simmer until mixture is reduced by half. Drizzle sauce over pork and serve.

Serves 6
Serve with Kendall-Jackson
Chardonnay

HOP KILN WINERY

The Hop Kiln is one of the most famous landmarks in Sonoma County. On the register of National Historic Trust Buildings, the Kiln, which was built around the turn of the century, has been the backdrop for four movies and now houses a fine, well-respected Sonoma County winery. Renovated by Dr. Martin Griffin in the mid-sixties, it celebrated its first crush in 1974. The winery is now the home to sixty-five acres of wine grapes that include Chardonnay, Gewürztraminer, Cabernet Sauvignon, and Valdiguié.

CRANBERRY
COUNTRY RIBS

*Because the preparations are done the day
before, this main course is ideal for patio
entertaining. Serve with dinner rolls and
fresh corn on the cob.*

3/4 cup canned whole cranberry sauce

8 cloves garlic, minced

2 tablespoons soy sauce

2 tablespoons Worcestershire sauce

2 tablespoons Hop Kiln Winery Zinfandel

2 pounds boneless country-style pork ribs

In the bowl of a food processor, combine cranberry sauce, garlic, soy sauce, Worcestershire sauce, and Zinfandel and process until smooth.

Lightly oil a baking pan just large enough to hold the ribs. Place ribs in pan and pour the cranberry mixture over the top. Cover and chill overnight.

Preheat oven to 350° F. Roast ribs for 1 hour, basting occasionally, until very tender. Skim off fat and serve with sauce spooned on top.

Serves 4
Serve with Hop Kiln Winery
Zinfandel

THE MONTELENA ESTATE
Cabernet Sauvignon
NAPA VALLEY
1991
GROWN, PRODUCED & ESTATE BOTTLED BY
CHATEAU MONTELENA WINERY, CALISTOGA, CALIFORNIA
ALCOHOL 14.01% BY VOLUME

CHATEAU MONTELENA WINERY

A visit to Chateau Montelena is a must for wine lovers seeking excellence. With thick natural stone walls, which maintain perfect temperature and humidity for aging wine, and the exceptional grapes that come from their Estate Vineyard, Chateau Montelena has earned its reputation as one of California's first growths. Even the French, for the first time in the history of winemaking, named the Chateau Montelena Chardonnay the world's greatest Chardonnay in 1976.

VENISON CHOPS MONTELENA

2 cups beef stock

1/4 cup crumbled dried porcini mushrooms

2 tablespoons butter

3 shallots, minced

2 tablespoons chopped oil-cured olives

1 teaspoon minced fresh marjoram

1 teaspoon minced fresh oregano

4 venison chops

Salt and freshly ground black pepper

1/4 cup olive oil

In a small saucepan, combine beef stock and porcini mushrooms. Bring to a boil, cover, and remove from heat. Let stand for 30 minutes to rehydrate mushrooms.

In a saucepan, melt butter over medium heat. Add shallots and sauté until tender. Add reserved mushrooms and stock, olives, marjoram, and oregano and simmer until liquid is reduced by half. Remove sauce from heat and keep warm.

Season venison well with salt and pepper. In a large cast-iron skillet, heat olive oil over medium-high heat. When the oil is almost smoking, add the venison chops and pan-fry until browned and crispy on both sides, and medium rare. Pour a little of the sauce over each chop and make sure that everyone gets some of the mushrooms and olives.

Serves 4
Serve with Chateau Montelena Winery
Cabernet Sauvignon

THE WINERIES:

Alderbrook Winery
2306 Magnolia Drive
Healdsburg, CA 95448
707.433.9154

Arrowood Vineyards & Winery
14347 Sonoma Highway
Glen Ellen, CA 95442
707.938.5170

Belvedere Vineyards and Winery
435 West Dry Creek Road
Healdsburg, CA 95448
707.433.8236

Beringer Vineyards
2000 Main Street
St. Helena, CA 94574
707.963.7115

Cakebread Cellars
8300 St. Helena Highway
Rutherford, CA 94573
707.963.5221

Cardinale
Post Office Box 328
Oakville, CA 94562
707.944.2807

Chateau Montelena Winery
1429 Tubbs Lane
Calistoga, CA 94515
707.942.5105

Clos Pegase Winery
1060 Dunaweal Lane
Calistoga, CA 94515
707.942.4981

Domaine Carneros
1240 Duhig Road
Napa, CA 94559
707.257.3020

Domaine Chandon
One California Drive
Yountville, CA 94599
707.944.2280

Dry Creek Vineyard
3770 Lambert Bridge Road
Healdsburg, CA 95448
707.433.1000

Duckhorn Vineyards
1000 Lodi Lane
St. Helena, CA 94574
707.963.7108

Frey Vineyards
14000 Tomki Road
Redwood Valley, CA 95470
707.485.5177

Frog's Leap Winery
8815 Conn Creek Road
Rutherford, CA 94573
707.963.4704

Geyser Peak Winery
22281 Chianti Road
Geyserville, CA 95441
707.857.9463

Gloria Ferrer Champagne Caves
23555 Highway 121
Sonoma, CA 95476
707.996.7256

Grgich Hills Cellar
1829 St. Helena Highway
Rutherford, CA 94573
707.963.2784

Hess Collection Winery
4411 Redwood Road
Napa, CA 94558
707.255.1144

Hop Kiln Winery
6050 Westside Road
Healdsburg, CA 95448
707.433.6491

Husch Vineyards
4400 Highway 128
Philo, CA 95466
707.462.5370

Joseph Phelps Vineyards
200 Taplin Road
St. Helena, CA 94574
707.963.2745

Kendall-Jackson Wine Center
5007 Fulton Road
Santa Rosa, CA 95439
707.571.8100

Kenwood Vineyards
9592 Sonoma Highway
Kenwood, CA 95452
707.833.5891

Korbel Champagne Cellars
13250 River Road
Guerneville, CA 95446
707.824.7000

Markham Vineyards
2812 St. Helena Highway
St. Helena, CA 94574
707.963.5292

Robert Mondavi Winery
7801 St. Helena Highway
Oakville, CA 94562
707.226.1395

Monticello Vineyards
4242 Big Ranch Road
Napa, CA 94558
800.743.6668

Navarro Vineyards
5601 Hwy 128
Philo, CA 95466
707.895.3686

Oakville Ranch Vineyards
    and Winery
7850 Silverado Trail
Oakville, CA 94562
707.944.9500

Parducci Wine Estates
501 Parducci Road
Ukiah, CA 95482
707.463.5350

Rodney Strong Vineyards
11455 Old Redwood Highway
Healdsburg, CA 95448
707.433.6521

Schweiger Vineyards and Winery
4015 Spring Mountain Road
St. Helena, CA 94574
707.963.4882

Shafer Vineyards
6154 Silverado Trail
Napa, CA 94558
707.944.9454

St. Supéry Vineyards and Winery
8440 St. Helena Highway
Rutherford, CA 94573
707.963.4507

Stone Creek Winery
9380 Sonoma Highway
Kenwood, CA 95452
707.833.4455

Sutter Home Winery
100 St. Helena Highway, South
St. Helena, CA 94574
707.963.3104

Topolos at Russian River
5700 Gravenstein Highway, North
Forestville, CA 95436
707.887.1575

Trefethen Vineyards
1160 Oak Knoll Avenue
Napa, CA 94558
707.255.7700

Turnbull Wine Cellars
8210 St. Helena Highway
Oakville, CA 94562
800.887.6285

V. Sattui Winery
1111 White Lane
St. Helena, CA 94574
707.963.7774

Viansa Winery
25200 Arnold Drive
Sonoma, CA 95476
707.935.4700

THE CATERERS:

Catering by Design
Post Office Box 1866
Glen Ellen, CA 95442
707.935.0390

Linda Thomas Catering
Napa Valley
707.944.8096

Vinga Restaurant
320 3rd Street
San Francisco, CA
415.546.3131

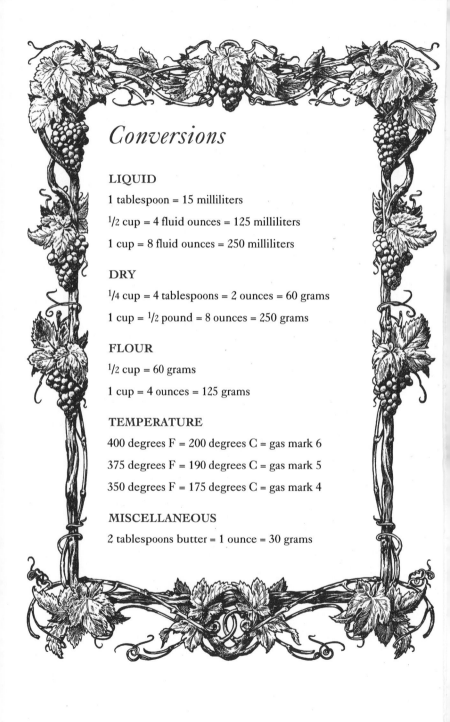

Conversions

LIQUID

1 tablespoon = 15 milliliters

$1/2$ cup = 4 fluid ounces = 125 milliliters

1 cup = 8 fluid ounces = 250 milliliters

DRY

$1/4$ cup = 4 tablespoons = 2 ounces = 60 grams

1 cup = $1/2$ pound = 8 ounces = 250 grams

FLOUR

$1/2$ cup = 60 grams

1 cup = 4 ounces = 125 grams

TEMPERATURE

400 degrees F = 200 degrees C = gas mark 6

375 degrees F = 190 degrees C = gas mark 5

350 degrees F = 175 degrees C = gas mark 4

MISCELLANEOUS

2 tablespoons butter = 1 ounce = 30 grams